D0579697

KITSAP REGIONAL LIBRARY

Tragic Fires Throughout History ™

The Triangle Shirtwaist Factory Fire of 1911

Janell Broyles

The Rosen Publishing Group, Inc., New York

To my dad, who was my first fan. I miss you.

Published in 2004 by The Rosen Publishing Group, Inc.
29 East 21st Street, New York, NY 10010

Copyright © 2004 by The Rosen Publishing Group, Inc.

First Edition

All rights reserved. No part of this book may be reproduced in any form without permission in writing from the publisher, except by a reviewer.

Library of Congress Cataloging-in-Publication Data

Broyles, Janell.
The Triangle Shirtwaist Factory fire of 1911 / by Janell Broyles. — 1st ed.
     p. cm. — (Tragic fires throughout history)
Summary: Describes the 1911 fire that destroyed New York City's Triangle Shirtwaist Factory and killed nearly one hundred and fifty workers, examining its causes and the reforms that came as a result of the tragedy. Includes bibliographical references and index.
ISBN 0-8239-4489-1 (library binding)
1. Triangle Shirtwaist Company—Fire, 1911—Juvenile literature. 2. New York (N.Y.)—History—1898–1951—Juvenile literature. 3. Clothing factories—New York (State)—New York—Safety measures—History—20th century—Juvenile literature. 4. Labor laws and legislation—New York (State)—New York—History—20th century—Juvenile literature. [1. Triangle Shirtwaist Company—Fire, 1911. 2. Industrial safety—History.] I. Title. II. Series.
 F128.5.B923 2004
 974.7'1041—dc22

                                                                    2003011785

Manufactured in the United States of America

CONTENTS

Introduction

Human beings have migrated in search of better lives since the dawn of time. The nomadic peoples of Asia, the ancestors of today's Native Americans, crossed over to North America thousands of years ago. But then the land bridges sank, and migration across the ocean from Asia or Europe became much more difficult. Even after the American Revolution, it was expensive and dangerous to cross the ocean, and immigration to the United States was a slow stream. But by the mid-nineteenth century, the invention of the steamship meant that ships could cross the ocean much more quickly and less expensively. Families in Europe and Asia could afford to travel to America, and they saw an opportunity to make new lives for themselves. The steady stream became a flood, and America's population exploded.

Upon reaching America, most of these immigrants lived in poverty, in crowded and filthy living conditions in New York City and other large cities. They took whatever jobs they could find, no matter what the pay and no matter what the working conditions. They came seeking the American dream, but first they had to survive.

With all their worldly possessions packed into duffel bags and suitcases, these immigrants enter New York City's Ellis Island in 1907. Immigrants processed on Ellis Island underwent physical examinations before being allowed to set foot on the mainland.

America's economy grew tremendously around the turn of the twentieth century, largely due to these immigrants. Ironically, although they were often despised, exploited, and ignored, their hard work in the factories of the United States created much of the nation's wealth.

As the economy grew, some business owners became more and more greedy, mostly at the expense of their immigrant laborers. Sweatshops employed hundreds of immigrants who worked long hours with little pay. Working conditions were poor, while health and safety measures were frequently overlooked by employers—all for the sake of saving money and increasing profits. Labor unions, which fought for workers' rights, were in their infancy and many politicians were as corrupt as the business owners. It seemed as though there was nothing that could be done to improve the lives and working conditions of immigrants. It was not until March 25, 1911, that America understood the high price these new citizens were paying for a chance at freedom and opportunity. For the first time, many Americans began to realize that it was a price that no society should ask.

On that afternoon in 1911, a small fire started on the eighth floor of the Triangle Shirtwaist Factory in New York City. The factory employed hundreds of immigrant workers to produce fashionable clothing at little pay. Like all sweatshops, there was little regard for the workers' safety. Doors were blocked to add workstations, fire escapes were poorly constructed in order to save money, and fire hoses were poorly maintained or not working

Monday's washing hangs out over the back alleys in turn-of-the-century New York City. Space was at a premium in tenement areas, as entire families were often crammed into small apartments.

altogether. Meanwhile, the factory was filled with cotton and linen, materials needed to produce the fashionable shirtwaists. These very materials would also be used to feed an inferno.

Just minutes after it began, the fire was out of control, racing from the eighth to the tenth floor of the factory building. In less than half an hour, it was all over. One hundred forty-six people—mostly young women, some as young as fourteen—were dead, victims of a system that valued their lives less than the profits of a greedy industry.

The Immigrants of New York

From the years 1820 to 1924, a great wave of immigrants—one of the greatest in history—flooded the shores of the United States. They came from Germany, Ireland, Norway, Sweden, Italy, Hungary, Russia, and every other country in Europe and Asia. They came because the old agricultural ways of life that had sustained their ancestors were breaking down. They came because famine and war had taken away their livelihoods. They came because prejudice and oppression put them in danger and limited their opportunities. They came because they hoped life in America would be better.

While many of these immigrants chose a rural farming life, a significant number stayed in the large cities of the East, especially New York. There were a number of reasons for this. First of all, many immigrants spent everything they had—or could borrow—to pay for their passage across the Atlantic. When they arrived, they had no money to buy wagons or livestock to continue their journey west across America.

Another reason was the ways in which immigrants managed to travel. Instead of a whole family immigrating together, a family would usually send one member, a son or daughter, over first. That member would have to find a job and a place to live, then begin sending as much money as possible back home. When enough was saved, a brother, sister, niece, or nephew might join the first member. Usually the new family member would live in the same place as his or her relative, as would everyone who followed. Soon, whole buildings and neighborhoods in New York City would be populated by families and friends from the same country or even the same village. This was called chain migration. Once they had found work and made a neighborhood their own, many immigrants were often reluctant to leave.

Finally, even if an immigrant found work and could send money home, he or she still lived on very little. The factories of New York, where most immigrants worked after the Industrial Revolution, paid just enough to keep them alive, but not enough for them to save up for a farm or anything else. Immigrants worked in dirty and, as we will see, dangerous factories. They lived in dark tenement buildings, sometimes with many people crammed into a few tiny rooms and without much in the way of plumbing or sanitation. Yet, because there was so much demand and because they were paid so little, even these rooms were expensive and most of their pay went toward rent. Landlords were often ruthless about throwing whole families out on the street because they could always find more tenants who could pay the rent.

Still, some of the newcomers managed to be successful. Many became factory owners themselves and, in turn, hired newer immigrants to work for them. The owners of the Triangle

First printed in 1880, this lithograph of a New York tenement has four floors labeled diphtheria, starvation, fever, and cholera. These ailments were common causes of death at the time, spread by the filthy conditions many poorer families were forced to live in.

Shirtwaist Company, the city's largest manufacturer of ladies' blouses, were Isaac Harris and Max Blanck, once immigrants themselves.

Other immigrants were thrifty and determined enough to scrimp and save for their children's sakes, thereby helping them have better lives. Many successful people were immigrants or the children of immigrants, including composer Irving Berlin, inventor Alexander Graham Bell, and millionaire industrialist Andrew Carnegie. It was success stories like these that continued to inspire people around the world to try their luck in the United States.

But in order to achieve such dreams, the newcomers had to survive long enough to succeed. In the factories and tenements of New York, the odds were often against them. The poor could not afford proper medical care during times of need. In the slums, poor sanitation and bad water led to outbreaks of terrible sicknesses such as cholera and dysentery.

FIRST STOP, ELLIS ISLAND

From 1892 to 1924, Ellis Island received thousands of new immigrants each day. After being checked for diseases and disabilities, each new arrival would be sent to the registry room, a great hall filled with immigrants. According to the Web site of the Ellis Island Immigration Museum, today, more than 100 million Americans can trace their family history back to a name in the inspector's record book in the registry room at Ellis Island.

A market along Manhattan's Hester Street, photographed in 1898, is busy with afternoon shoppers. The gradual mixing of cultures over time has made New York one of the most ethnically diverse cities in the United States, if not the world.

In the winter, many buildings lacked heat, and some people would freeze to death. Or else they would start illegal fires in their rooms to keep warm and possibly set a whole block ablaze.

Some of the better-off citizens of New York tried to help those in the slums, or poorer areas. Many charities sought to help the poor receive medical attention, food, and shelter. But the government, which saw the poor as a minor problem, offered them little help, and the sheer number of immigrants pouring into the city made it impossible for charities to help them all.

Warnings Ignored

Isaac Harris and Max Blanck were an American success story. According to Leon Stein in his book *The Triangle Fire*, the two men were known as the Shirtwaist Kings for their domination of the shirtwaist market in New York. A shirtwaist is a woman's blouse, tailored to be worn with a long skirt, a style of dress that was fashionable in the early twentieth century. They were inexpensive and practical to wear, and so they became very popular, especially among working women, who needed plain, comfortable clothes.

A Profitable System

Like many other shrewd businessmen, Harris and Blanck had a profitable system to keep their workers' productivity high and costs low. According to Stein, the laws at the time specified that each worker be provided with "250 cubic feet of air." This meant that factories were built with high ceilings to give workers the required air space, but workers were still crowded together, generally at a long table of sewing machines. Women sat in

Max Blanck and Isaac Harris came out of an eighteen-day trial acquitted of all responsibility. Sued by twenty-three families, they would end up paying a settlement equal to about $75 per death. *Above right:* This shirtwaist is similar to those assembled in Blanck and Harris's factory.

staggered rows on each side of the table so that they had room in front of them to move their sewing under the machine. For light they relied on windows or dim gas lamps.

Harris and Blanck didn't hire their workers themselves. Instead, they had a system that kept them from having much responsibility for their workers under the law. Harris and Blanck would hire a contractor—an experienced sewing machine operator—who would be assigned a half-dozen machines. The contractor would then usually hire immigrants from his or her homeland at a low learner's rate. The contractor never told them what he or she was getting paid by the company or what the other workers in the factory were making. Even after the immigrant workers became experienced sewers, the contractor would often keep paying them the low rate. The contractor and the Triangle Shirtwaist Company would then keep the difference in pay. In addition, workers could also have deductions in their pay for various things. These could be fees for needles, the chairs they sat in, the lockers where they stored their clothes, and any materials they accidentally spoiled. The company payroll listed only the contractors, not the workers they hired, so Triangle never knew exactly how many people were working for them.

Every Saturday, the contractors paid their workers, using whatever system they saw fit. There was no fixed rate for the work, and a worker could get less pay just because the contractor had taken a dislike to him or her. At the same time, contractors were being pressured by their bosses to pay as little as possible in order to keep profits high.

Creating a Firetrap

Fire safety laws did exist in 1911, but they were not well enforced, and they concentrated more on keeping a building from burning than on getting occupants out safely. The Asch Building, which housed the Triangle Shirtwaist Company, was fairly modern and was in fact fireproof, in the sense that it would probably remain standing after a fire. It was also incredibly dangerous for the people who worked inside it.

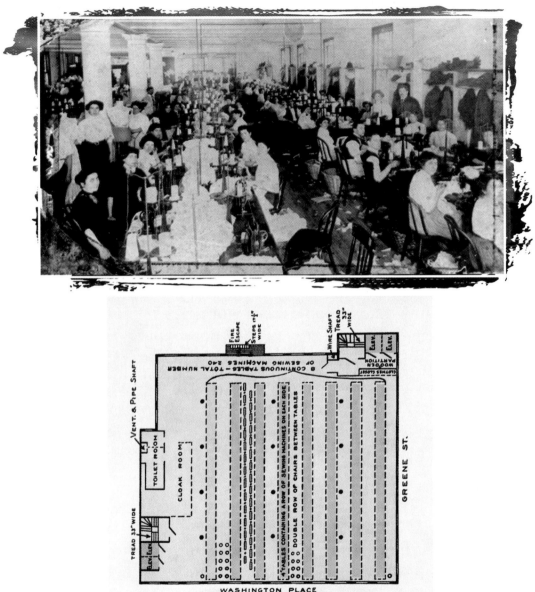

A diagram of the ninth floor of the Triangle Shirtwaist Factory *(bottom)* shows how crowded the workrooms were. Workers were seldom allowed to move around or even go to the bathroom, and their days were filled with repetitive drudgery, as seen in this photograph of a typical sweatshop of the era *(top)*.

Linen and cotton, the main materials used for women's shirtwaists, are very flammable—more so than paper. Huge rolls of these materials were always in the Triangle Factory, along with bins full of scraps left over from cutting out shirts. In addition, highly flammable oil was used to keep each sewing machine greased and working. Underneath the sewing machine, a wooden tray was attached to the table, just above a sewer's knees, to catch the oil when it dripped.

But the most outrageous safety hazard at the Triangle Factory was the construction of the building itself. Joseph J. Asch, the building's owner, cut corners in order to save money during the building's construction. First, it was built 135 feet (41 meters) tall. Had there been one extra story, making it 150 feet (46 m) tall, the city would have required metal trim on the outside, metal window frames, and stone or concrete floors. By keeping it shorter, Asch saved quite a bit by having wooden—and thus flammable—trim, frames, and floors instead.

Even at that lower height, the building was supposed to have three interior staircases, instead of just the two that were actually built. But constant bickering among architects, business owners, and building inspectors meant that this was never enforced. And although the city pointed out that the fire escape on the outside of the building was outdated and poorly constructed, no action was ever taken to force Asch to fix the problem. In fact, neither outside fire escapes nor indoor sprinklers were required by law at that time, again due to

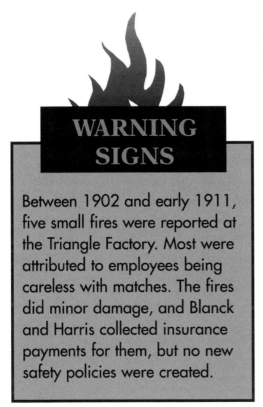

WARNING SIGNS

Between 1902 and early 1911, five small fires were reported at the Triangle Factory. Most were attributed to employees being careless with matches. The fires did minor damage, and Blanck and Harris collected insurance payments for them, but no new safety policies were created.

pressure from factory owners, who did not want to spend the money to install them. In addition, there was no law requiring fire drills in factories—drills that would teach workers the quickest way out of the building in case of an emergency.

The Fight for Better Conditions

The International Ladies Garment Workers' Union was formed in 1900 to help workers demand better pay and safer conditions. Fearful that empowered workers would demand more money and cut into their profits, garment manufacturers did everything they could to prevent their workers from joining a union.

The International Ladies Garment Workers' Union organized workers in the women's clothing trade. Many of the garment workers before 1911 were unorganized, partly because they were mostly young immigrant women. But in 1909, an incident at the Triangle Shirtwaist Factory sparked a spontaneous walkout by its 400 employees. The Women's Trade Union League, a progressive association of middle-class women (including Anne Morgan, daughter of wealthy industrialist J. P. Morgan), helped the workers picket and defend themselves against strikebreakers and police abuse. Garment workers all over the city joined, until there were more than 20,000 strikers demanding better pay and conditions. But cold weather and lack of funds ended the strike in a few months.

Braving the cold and the threat of violence from brutal strikebreakers, these garment workers walk the picket line in February 1910. The strike was known as the Uprising of the 20,000, and it marked a turning point in the history of organized labor in America.

The next year, however, a cloak makers' strike led to a historic agreement (the Protocol of Peace) that established a system to eliminate problems in the garment industry. Unfortunately for the workers, though, many shops were still in the hands of unfair owners—such as Blanck and Harris—who had little regard for basic workers' rights. Still, no changes were made at the Triangle Factory to improve safety or working conditions. On March 25, 1911, the whole country would witness the tragic result.

Inferno

At 4:45 PM on March 25, 1911, the quitting bell rang at the Triangle Factory. One of the employees, Joseph Granick, had just received his pay and was walking toward one of the exits when Eva Harris, the sister of owner Isaac Harris, ran up to him. She told him she smelled something burning. In *The Triangle Fire*, Granick recalled, "I looked to the cutting tables. At the second table, through the slot under the top, I saw the red flames." Some of the cutters began throwing pails of water on the flames. But the blaze was already too big.

The Eighth Floor—The Fire Starts

Cloth shirtwaist patterns hung on wires above the cutting table on the eighth floor of the Asch Building. Soon they began to burn, and tiny pieces of burning fabric flew off and settled all around the shop, spreading the fire. A large sewing table caught fire, and the flames were growing taller. The blaze began to feed on the tables, the floors, and the wooden trim around the windows. As the heat built up, windows popped and shattered.

A worker named William Bernstein suddenly remembered there were fire hoses in the stairwell. Bernstein and another worker ran to get the hoses, but when they tried to turn them on, they wouldn't work. "No pressure. No water. I tried it. I opened it. I turned the nozzle one way and then another. It didn't work. I threw it away," he recalled later in *The Triangle Fire*. Several other employees tried to make the hoses work, without success.

One of the back windows on the eighth floor faced the fire escape, and several workers managed to force it open and clamber out. Meanwhile, others crowded into the freight elevators and stairways on the Greene Street and Washington Place sides of the factory.

In a corner of the shop, phone operator Dinah Lifschitz stayed at her desk and tried desperately to call the ninth and tenth floors. She got through to warn the people on

'FOR GOD'S SAKE, STOP!'

Just as the eighth-floor workers began ringing desperately for the elevators, the executives on the tenth floor did the same. The elevator operators were passing the people on the eighth floor to get to those on the tenth! In *The Triangle Fire*, worker Irene Seivos recalled, "Some of the girls were clawing at the elevator doors and crying, 'Stop! Stop! For God's sake, stop!' I broke the window of the elevator door with my hands and screamed 'Fire! Fire! Fire!' It was so hot we could scarcely breathe. When the elevator did stop and the door opened at last, my dress was catching fire."

These horse-drawn fire engines rush toward the fire at the Triangle Shirtwaist Company. The fire hoses they carried would not have enough pressure for water to reach the blaze on the eighth and ninth floors.

the tenth floor—where the Triangle executives worked—but there was no answer on the ninth. Lifschitz then called the police, who alerted the fire department.

With the elevators so crowded, many girls rushed to the staircases. But since the doors had been designed to open inward instead of out, the crush of people against the doors made them impossible to open. On the Washington Place side, a supervisor named Louis Brown managed to push enough people back to wedge the door open, and they all squeezed out and desperately began climbing down the narrow, twisting staircases. Many fainted, were trampled, or were burned by the approaching flames. Those left behind, cut off from both exits by smoke and fire, crawled out onto the windowsills, but could not escape the flames that shot out along the ledges. Although the onlookers below yelled at them not to jump, they chose to leap to their deaths rather than be burned alive. They would not be the last.

The Tenth Floor—The Lucky Few

The tenth floor of the Asch Building housed the executive offices, some garment pressers, and those who handled packing and shipping. There were about seventy people there that day, but they were very fortunate and lost only one worker to the fire, a young girl who panicked and jumped out of the window instead of trying to escape safely. Once they were warned by the phone call from the eighth floor, they began calling elevators and gathering up important account books. At first, it was all very calm, but as the flames and smoke began to filter up from the floors below—and as the elevators became unable to keep up with the demand—those who remained realized they were in danger.

Three of those who discovered they would not be able to use the elevators were Max Blanck and his two young daughters, twelve-year-old Henrietta and five-year-old Mildred. Edward N. Markowitz, who was in charge of shipping, saw the Blancks standing somewhat bewildered in the center of the floor, and he took charge of them. "I went over to Mr. Blanck and told him, 'The only way you can get out is over the roof. But you better be quick about it!'" Markowitz recalled in *The Triangle Fire*. The Blancks and the remaining employees struggled up the Greene Street stairs to the roof, singed by flames that were coming in through the stairwell windows from the floors below.

Although some workers from the other floors had made it to the roof only to jump in their panic, the rest were now being helped by some New York University students. The students laid painters' ladders from their windows across the alley to the Asch Building, allowing the workers to crawl to safety.

The Ninth Floor—No Warning, No Escape

Max Hochfield and his sister Esther normally worked on the eighth floor, but had been assigned to the ninth that week. Too impatient to wait for Esther, Max was the first out of the door and down the stairs when the quitting bell rang, and he was the first from the ninth floor to see the fire. He started to go back up to get his sister, only to be stopped by a fireman who had come up the stairs. "I shouted at him, 'I have to save my sister!'" Max remembered in *The Triangle Fire*. "But he turned me around and ordered me, 'Go down, if you want to stay alive!'" Max would make it out, but he would never see his sister again.

The employees on the Asch Building's ninth floor had the worst chance for escape. Having no warning by telephone, they only discovered the flames beneath them when it was already too late to escape easily. "All of a sudden the fire was all around," said survivor

The fire escape *(left)* was not strong enough to bear the weight of the dozens of workers who climbed on it, hoping to escape the deadly blaze. The building's elevator *(right)* was also of little help to those trapped by the fire.

Rose Glantz in *The Triangle Fire*. "The flames were coming in through many of the windows." Workers rushed to the Washington Place stairway doors, only to find them locked. Many died there, clawing at the locked door, unable to move because of the panicked, confused crowd crushing them against the door and the flames that moved with terrible speed. Glantz and some others managed to break away and make it down the Greene Street stairway by running through the flames. They were the lucky ones.

A few workers remembered the fire escape at the rear of the building. Nellie Ventura and a group of other women banged at the

WITNESS TO A TRAGEDY

Reporter William Shepherd of United Press International had been one of the first on the scene, and he stayed until its grim finish. According to the Cornell University's Web site on the Triangle fire, he wrote, "I looked upon the heap of dead bodies and I remembered these girls were shirtwaist makers. I remembered their great strike last year in which the same girls had demanded more sanitary conditions and more safety precautions in the shops. These dead bodies were the answer."

metal shutters until they forced them open. Then they stepped out the window and onto the balcony. Thick smoke and fire were already streaming out below them on the eighth-floor balcony. "At first I was too frightened," Ventura recalled in *The Triangle Fire*. "Then I heard the screams of the girls inside. I knew I had to go down the ladder or die where I was."

Ventura was one of the fortunate few to even make it down the escape. Another survivor, Abe Gordon, recalled that he felt the fire escape was weakening. At the sixth floor, he ducked back inside the building through a window. In *The Triangle Fire*, Gordon said, "I still had one foot on the fire escape when I heard a loud noise and looked back up. The people were falling all around me, screaming all around me. The fire escape was collapsing."

On the ninth floor, time was running out. The fire escape was gone, crowds blocked the freight elevators, and the way down on the Greene Street side was cut off by flames. The only place left to go was up the Greene Street stairs to the roof, provided you could make it through the flames. Many were singed and burned as they wrapped shawls or fabric around themselves and plunged through fire to escape.

The flames had trapped the remaining workers between the long horizontal rows of burning tables and against the locked door to Washington Place. The tiny passenger elevators still got a few to safety, but they were too small to get all the workers out before the flames and smoke consumed them. Soon even the elevators could make no more trips—flames from the eighth and ninth floors had begun filling the elevator shafts too. Slowly, the doomed Triangle workers were pushed to the windows by the fire. They climbed up

Despite the fact that it was gutted by the fire, the Asch Building still stands today in lower Manhattan. The building is now known as New York University's Brown Building.

and out onto the windowsills, but the fire was billowing out of the windows, burning the wooden trim, leaving no place to escape. As the flames licked at their hair and clothing, they began, alone and in small groups, to jump.

Horrified New Yorkers watched from the streets. Fire trucks had arrived, but could do little. The ladders and hoses could not

Many workers leapt to their deaths rather than suffer the fate of being burned alive. At this point, there was nothing anyone could do to help the workers trapped in the building.

reach higher than the sixth floor. Those who jumped gathered such speed as they fell that blankets and nets wouldn't hold them; they smashed through to the pavement below. Again and again the crowd watched as victims leaped or fell to their deaths. The smell of blood startled the fire horses, and the police and firemen had difficulty getting around the bodies to train their hoses on the building. No one who jumped survived.

As quickly as it began, it was over. In less than half an hour, the Triangle Shirtwaist Factory fire had claimed 146 lives.

Aftermath

In the weeks after the fire, New York mourned its dead. A special morgue had to be set up on the East River pier so that relatives could come and claim the bodies of their loved ones. Many bodies were so burned that only a piece of clothing or jewelry allowed families to identify them. After three days, all but seven of the bodies had been claimed, and on April 5, a mass funeral was held for the last seven victims. About 120,000 people followed the hearses through New York City, and 400,000 more watched from the sidewalks and streets.

Who Was to Blame?

In the wake of the tragedy, shocked and angry New Yorkers demanded to know how this could have happened. How could a fire take so many innocent lives? Why didn't more of the workers escape? Immediately, the papers and workers' unions set their sights on Blanck and Harris. The refusal of the Triangle Shirtwaist Company to honor the Protocol of Peace, the brutal attacks on

Firemen on horseback lead this trade union procession under the arch in Washington Square Park in lower Manhattan. More than 120,000 people followed the hearses that carried the bodies of the workers through the streets. It was a day of mourning for the entire city.

protesters who demanded better conditions, and the testimony of those who survived damned the two men in the eyes of the public.

That's why it was so shocking when both Blanck and Harris, after a lengthy and sensational trial, were acquitted of any wrongdoing. Prosecutors were unable to prove that they had knowingly let the doors be locked. The other dangers in the Asch Building—the fire escapes, the malfunctioning extinguishers— were either not illegal or were considered accidents, not intentional negligence. It did not help that many agencies—the building department, the borough of Manhattan, and the fire department—all pointed fingers at one another, attempting to deflect blame. The truth was, the laws that existed were inadequate and seldom enforced, and the system itself was corrupt and underfunded. There were not enough inspectors, and they had little power to penalize businesses or landlords.

A week after the fire, the Triangle Shirtwaist Company reopened in a new building, and fire inspectors found that sewing machines had been set up in such a way that they blocked the exits. Something had to change.

Unfortunately, as long as the government sided with men like Blanck and Harris, change seemed to be a hopeless task. Still, the pressure was building. Papers like the *New York Tribune* and the *New York World* kept the story alive, reporting on the devastation of families who had lost breadwinners and loved ones, asking questions about the corruption of the system that had led to the tragedy. The mood was shifting, and in Albany, the capital of New York, powerful people in the government were beginning to take notice.

Fireproof, but Still a Trap

To understand just how so many died on the day of the Triangle fire, it's important to know what obstacles prevented the workers from getting out.

The three main escape routes were staircases and freight elevators on the Washington Place and Greene Street sides and a fire escape

RECORD FIRE
FOR NEW YORK
145
LIVES LOST!!!
BUILDING FIRE PROOF
ONLY FIRE ESCAPE
COLLAPSED.
OUR INSPECTOR

The horror that people felt at the terrible toll of the fire is expressed in this cartoon, depicting a building inspector as a grinning skeleton.

that came down in the north courtyard. On a normal day, workers would leave on the Washington Place side, where their managers would check their bags for stolen items and give them their pay on paydays. The landings outside each floor were too narrow to allow the doors to the stairs to open out, so they only opened inwards. The law stated only that doors had to open out when it was "practicable." Having a staircase too narrow to let a door open outward wasn't illegal.

Then there was the matter of the locked doors. Several employees were unable to open the Washington Place side doors on the ninth floor, although those on the eighth were opened. It was illegal but not uncommon for employers to keep stair doors locked to prevent union organizers from coming into the shops or employees from stealing goods. According to *The Triangle Fire*, in 1909, fire inspector P. J. McKeon found that the door to the Washington Place staircase was "usually kept locked" to help "keep track of so

The Triangle Factory was completely destroyed after the fire. Two hundred forty sewing machines were crowded on the ninth floor alone, and the tables were so close together that workers were climbing over them in an attempt to escape.

many girls." Blanck and Harris maintained that they did not lock the doors. Regardless, once panic set in and the workers began crowding against the doors trying to get out, they were trapped, because the doors opened inward. Those who escaped were those who made it into the freight elevators or were close enough to the doors to get out first.

As a way out, the fire escape was a deadly failure. Many of the workers didn't even know it existed. It could be reached only

A building inspector, sorting through the ruins of the factory, points to a locked door. By locking the doors, the factory owners would be able to keep workers from sneaking out while preventing union representatives from sneaking in. This practice would also turn the factory into a death trap.

through rusty metal shutters that were difficult to open. In addition, the shutters opened outward, so workers coming down from the ninth floor found themselves blocked by the eighth-floor shutters. The escape itself was weak and rickety. As the panicked workers crowded onto it, it finally collapsed beneath them and sent them to their deaths. Only twenty workers made it down the escape before it fell.

The Legacy of a Tragedy

The key to changing New York's laws lay with the New York State legislature. And the key to the legislature lay with Charles Francis Murphy, the boss of Tammany Hall. Originally founded as a social club, Tammany Hall controlled most of the Democratic Party in New York during much of the late nineteenth and early twentieth centuries. Although it relied on the votes of immigrants and the working class, it had a history of corruption and greed, including being bribed by wealthy businessmen. Tammany had not supported the unions and strikers, using its influence to help the wealthy and powerful textile manufacturers instead.

But Tammany was being challenged by Democrats as well as Republicans, and anger over the Triangle fire ran deep among the immigrant voters Tammany depended on. Murphy, a man of so few words he was known as Silent Charlie, decided it was time to push for reform, or improvements. He appointed two of his protégés, Robert F. Wagner and Albert E. Smith, to head up a new statewide Factory Investigating Commission. The commission's

Robert F. Wagner *(left)* and Al Smith *(right)* headed the Factory Investigating Commission. They were responsible for numerous reforms in workplace safety laws.

members also included the renowned labor leader Samuel Gompers and labor activist Frances Perkins, who had been one of the onlookers as the Triangle workers jumped to their deaths.

The social reformers who had been trying for years to improve life for the poor workers of New York had little faith in this new movement. They had seen many politicians and prominent citizens make grand speeches about helping the working people, only to betray them. They didn't trust the new commission, and they regarded Al Smith with suspicion.

Meanwhile, the factory owners, believing that Tammany was still on their side, didn't pay much attention to the reformers. They had gotten used to getting their way in the legislature, and they thought Smith would follow the path of those before him by not pushing for reform.

Both sides were wrong.

Al Smith Takes On the System

Born in 1873, Smith grew up in the shadow of the construction of the Brooklyn Bridge. The son of an Irish teamster, Smith had known terrible poverty and had been working since the age of thirteen. Years later, he was proud of saying he had only one degree, F.F.M.—for the Fulton Fish Market, where he worked as a day laborer to support his family. He entered politics by becoming an errand runner for a local politician, and by the age of twenty-eight, he was the majority leader of the New York State Assembly.

When the commission finally began to make its recommendations, Smith had won over those who doubted him. "You make the proposals. I'll fight for them," he said, according to *New York: An Illustrated Story*. In three sessions of the New York legislature, between 1912 and 1914, Smith pushed through one reform bill after another. Then he sent them to the state senate, where his fellow Tammany member, Robert Wagner, made sure they became laws.

These historic laws had a profound impact on the lives of workers. Factory owners were now required to provide enclosed staircases, sprinklers, adequate lighting and ventilation, washrooms, and first-aid kits. Machinery would be regulated if it posed any danger to workers. Women would not be allowed to work more than fifty-four hours a week, and children under fourteen would not be allowed to work in factories at all. In all, the

FRANCES PERKINS

Frances Perkins was the head of the New York Consumers' League, which lobbied for better working hours and conditions. Perkins and other labor leaders met with Al Smith, and with his help, the Factory Investigating Commission was created. After the state passed the laws Smith pushed through, Perkins felt that the state in some way "had paid the debt society owed to those children, those young people who lost their lives in the Triangle Fire," according to the Social Security Administration Web site.

But the Triangle fire's legacy would influence Perkins all of her professional life. She became an aide to Franklin D. Roosevelt when he was governor of New York, and after Roosevelt became president in 1932, she became his secretary of labor. Perkins was the first woman in United States history to hold a cabinet position.

Perkins played a key role writing New Deal legislation, including minimum-wage laws and the Social Security Act of 1935. Perkins believed Roosevelt's New Deal was a response to tragedies such as the Triangle fire. The Social Security Administration Web site quotes Perkins as saying, "[The New Deal] was based really upon the experiences that we had had in New York State and upon the sacrifices of those who, we faithfully remember with affection and respect, died in that terrible fire on March 25, 1911. They did not die in vain and we will never forget them."

In 1945, Perkins was asked by President Harry S. Truman to serve on the U.S. Civil Service Commission, which she did until her retirement in 1952. Perkins continued to be active as a teacher and lecturer until her death on May 14, 1965.

President Franklin D. Roosevelt *(seated)* signs the Social Security Act into law in 1935. Part of Roosevelt's New Deal, social security was one of the many reforms that helped the nation through the Great Depression. Frances Perkins is pictured to the right of President Roosevelt.

Factory Investigating Commission made sixty recommendations, and fifty-four became laws. New York State now had the most humane and liberal factory laws in the United States.

The changes didn't stop there. Many members of the commission went on to hold positions of influence in New York and in Washington, D.C., and the reforms they supported were eventually installed nationwide. In 1918, Al Smith himself became governor of New York and later ran for president of the United States, losing to Franklin D. Roosevelt.

Anti-sweatshop activists take to the streets of New York on December 11, 2002. There are still millions of people around the world, many of them children, who labor under unfair and dangerous working conditions.

Safety in the Twenty-first Century

While the laws passed in 1914 made a real difference in the lives of factory workers in the United States, there are many who say that keeping workers safe is an ongoing battle.

According to Cornell University's Web site on the Triangle fire, sweatshops have not yet disappeared in the United States. Recent studies conducted by the U.S. Department of Labor found that 67 percent of Los Angeles garment factories and 63 percent of New York garment factories violate minimum wage and overtime laws.

Ninety-eight percent of Los Angeles garment factories have workplace health and safety problems serious enough to lead to severe injuries or death.

The Revolutionary Worker's Web site reports that illegal or badly policed sweatshop districts in the United States have conditions that approach those of the Triangle Factory. During a 1991 fire, twenty-five workers died behind locked doors in Hamlet, North Carolina, in a chicken-processing plant that had no sprinklers or fire alarms.

As in 1911, those who take on the dirty and dangerous work in factories are largely the poor or new immigrants, people willing to do what they must to survive. Human nature hasn't changed much since 1911, and some businesses still take advantage of their workers when they can. Although the laws to protect workers are in place, sometimes it takes pressure on politicians and governments from unions, consumer groups, and informed voters to make sure they're enforced. That responsibility belongs to all of us.

Timeline

January 15, 1901
Asch Building is completed.

April 1902
The Triangle Shirtwaist Company moves into the eighth, ninth, and tenth floors of the Asch Building.

1908
Triangle Shirtwaist production reaches $1 million mark.

November 23, 1909
Triangle workers strike for better conditions and are eventually joined by 20,000 garment workers from around New York City.

March 1910
The strike ends.

September 1910
Cloak makers' strike forces many factory owners to sign the Protocol of Peace.

March 25, 1911
The Triangle Factory burns.

June 30, 1911
Charles Murphy appoints Al Smith and Robert F. Wagner to the Factory Investigating Commission.

December 4, 1911
Trial of Max Blanck and Isaac Harris begins.

December 27, 1911
Blanck and Harris are found not guilty of locking exit doors in the Triangle Factory.

1912–1914
Factory Investigating Commission creates dozens of new laws regulating factory conditions and employment in New York State

March 26, 2003
The Asch Building, now owned by New York University, is declared a New York City landmark by Mayor Michael R. Bloomberg, in honor of the Triangle fire victims.

Glossary

calamity (kuh-LAH-mih-tee) A disaster or misfortune.

day laborer (DAY LAY-bor-er) One who works for a day's wage, usually an unskilled worker.

empower (em-POW-ur) To give one power to do something.

flammable (FLAM-uh-bul) Something that easily catches on fire.

galvanize (GAL-vun-IZE) To strengthen.

humane (HEW-mane) Consideration or sympathy for humans or animals.

Industrial Revolution (in-DUS-tree-ul reh-vuh-LOO-shun) The period of time in the mid- to late-nineteenth century when manufacturing became increasingly centralized and mechanized.

labor union (LAY-bor YOON-yun) An organization of workers dedicated to advancing its members' interests.

lobbying (LAH-bee-ing) Attempting to influence a public official to change laws.

New Deal (NOO DEEL) A program of social reform and economic recovery promoted by President Franklin D. Roosevelt in the 1930s.

protégé (PRO-teh-zhay) One who is trained, supported, or sponsored by another.

protocol (PROH-toh-kall) A document or record that describes an agreement between two or more parties.

strikebreaker (STRIHK-bray-kur) A person hired to replace a striking worker.

sweatshops (SWET-shops) Factories that force employees to work in dangerous or illegal conditions.

teamster (TEEM-stur) Someone who drives a team of horses or, nowadays, a truck.

tenement (TEN-uh-ment) A building with many floors and with many families living on each level.

For More Information

Lower East Side Tenement Museum
90 Orchard Street
New York, NY 10002
Web site: http://www.tenement.org

The Museum of the City of New York
1220 Fifth Avenue at 103rd Street
New York, NY 10029
Web site: http://www.mcny.org

UNITE!
1710 Broadway
New York, NY 10019
Web site: http://www.uniteunion.org

Web Sites

Due to the changing nature of Internet links, the Rosen Publishing Group, Inc., has developed an online list of Web sites related to the subject of this book. This site is updated regularly. Please use this link to access the list:

http://www.rosenlinks.com/tfth/tsff

For Further Reading

Bader, Bonnie. *East Side Story*. New York: Silver Moon Press, 1993.

Burns, Ric, James Sanders, and Lisa Ades. *New York: An Illustrated History*. New York: Alfred A. Knopf, 1999.

Daniels, Roger. *Coming to America: A History of Immigration and Ethnicity in American Life*. New York: HarperPerennial, 2002.

Dash, Joan. *We Shall Not Be Moved: The Women's Factory Strike of 1909*. New York: Scholastic, Inc., 1996.

De Angelis, Gina. *The Triangle Shirtwaist Company Fire of 1911*. Philadelphia: Chelsea House Publishers, 2001.

Diamond, Barbara Goldin. *Fire*. New York: Viking, 1992.

Ellis, Edward Robb. *The Epic of New York City*. New York: Kodansha America, Inc., 1997.

Littlefield, Holly. *Fire at the Triangle Factory*. Minneapolis: Carolrhoda Books, 1996.

Sherrow, Victoria. *The Triangle Factory Fire*. Brookfield, CT: Millbrook Press, 1995.

Stein, Leon. *The Triangle Fire*. New York: Carroll & Graf Publishers, Inc., 1962.

Von Drehle, David. *Triangle: The Fire That Changed America*. New York: Atlantic Monthly Press, 2003.

Bibliography

Burns, Ric, James Sanders, and Lisa Ades. *New York: An Illustrated History*. New York: Alfred A. Knopf, 1999.

Christian, Nichole M. "A Landmark of the Unspeakable; Honoring the Site Where 146 Died in the Triangle Shirtwaist Fire." *New York Times*, March 26, 2003.

Daniels, Roger. *Coming to America: A History of Immigration and Ethnicity in American Life*. New York: HarperPerennial, 2002.

Ellis, Edward Robb. *The Epic of New York City*. New York: Kodansha America, Inc., 1997.

Ellis Island Immigration Museum Web site. Retrieved April 3, 2003 (http://www.ellisisland.com).

"Frances Perkins." Social Security Administration Web site. Retrieved April 3, 2003 (http://www.ssa.gov/history/fperkins.html).

"Housing." Columbia Encyclopedia Online, Sixth Edition, 2001. Retrieved April 3, 2003 (http://www.bartleby.com/65/ho/housing.html).

Rosa, Paul. "The Triangle Shirtwaist Fire." Historybuff.com Web site. Retrieved April 3, 2003 (http://www.historybuff.com/library/refshirtwaist.html).

Stein, Leon. *The Triangle Fire*. New York: Carroll & Graf Publishers, Inc., 1962.

"Tammany." Columbia Encyclopedia Online, Sixth Edition, 2001. Accessed April 3, 2003 (http://www.bartleby.com/65/ta/Tammany.html).

Triangle Factory Fire Web site. Cornell University. Retrieved April 3, 2003 (http://www.ilr.cornell.edu/trianglefire).

"The Women of the Triangle Fire." *Revolutionary Worker*, Issue 1046, March 12, 2000.

Index

About the Author

Janell Broyles is a writer and editor, originally from Texas, who now lives in New York City. She has always been interested in history and has written for both print and online magazines. This is her first book for young adults.

Photo Credits

Cover, p. 1 © Underwood & Underwood/Corbis; pp. 5, 19, 22, 30, 39 Library of Congress Prints and Photographs Division; p. 7 © Hulton/Archive/Getty Images; pp. 10, 25 (right), 34, 36 © Bettmann/Corbis; p. 12 © Museum of the City of New York, The Byron Collection; pp. 14 (left), 16, 32 UNITE Archives, Kheel Center, Cornell University, Ithaca, NY; p. 14 (right) National Museum of American History, Smithsonian Institution; pp. 25 (left), 27, 28, 33 Brown Brothers; p. 40 © AP/Wide World Photos.

Designer: Les Kanturek; Editor: Charles Hofer; Photo Researcher: Amy Feinberg